Melito of Sardis

Melito of Sardis

[a.d. 160-170-177.] Melito may have been the immediate successor of the "angel" (or "apostle") of the church of Sardis, to whom our Great High Priest addressed one of the apocalyptic messages. He was an "Apostolic Father" in point of fact; he very probably knew the blessed Polycarp and his disciple Irenaeus. He is justly revered for the diligence with which he sought out the evidence which, in his day, established the Canon of the Old Testament, then just complete.

In the following fragments we find him called Bishop of Sardis, Bishop of Ittica, and Bishop of Ittica. He is also introduced to us as "the Philosopher," and we shall find him styled "the Eunuch" by Polycrates. It is supposed that he had made himself a coelebs "for the kingdom of heaven's sake," without mistaking our Lord's intent, as did Origen. He was not a monk, but accepted a single estate to be the more free and single-eyed in the Master's service. From the encyclopedic erudition of Lightfoot we glean some particulars, as follows:-

1. I have adopted his date, as Lightfoot gives it,-that is, the period of his writings,-under the Antonines. The improbability of seventy years in the episcopate is reason enough for rejecting the idea that he was himself the "angel of the church of Sardis," to whom our Lord sent the terrible rebuke.

2. His silence concerning persecutions under Vespasian, Trojan, and Antoninus Pius cannot be pleaded to exempt them from this stain, against positive evidence to the contrary.

3. A coincidence with Ignatius to the Ephesians will be noted hereafter.

4. Melito, with Claudius Apollinaris and even Polycrates, may have been personally acquainted with Ignatius; of course, one with another. These lived not far from Smyrna; Asia Minor was, in the first century, the focus of Christian activity.

5. We know of his visit to the East from his own account, preserved by Eusebius. The Christians of proconsular Asia were accustomed to such journeys. Even Clement of Alexandria may have met him, as he seems to have met Tatian and Theodotus.

6. Melito vouches for the rescript of Hadrian, but his supposed reference to the edict of Antoninus does not bear close scrutiny as warrant for its authenticity.

7. The Apology of our author was addressed to Aurelius in his mid-career as a sovereign, about a.d. 170. Justin, Melito, Athenagoras, and Theophilus all tell the same sad story of imperial cruelty. Even when Justin wrote to Antoninus, Marcus was supreme in the councils of the elder emperor.

8. He became a martyr, probably under Marcus Aurelius, *circa* a.d.177; some eminent critics have even dated his Apology as late as this.

I.
- A Discourse Which Was in the Presence of Antoninus Caesar, and He Exhorted The Said Caesar to Acquaint Himself with God, and Showed to Him the Way of Truth.

He began to speak as follows:-

"It is not easy," said Melito, "speedily to bring into the right way the man who has a long time previously been held fast by error. It may, however, be effected: for, when a man turns away ever so little from error, the mention of the truth is acceptable to him. For, just as when the cloud breaks ever so little there comes fair weather, even so, when a man turns toward God, the thick cloud of error which deprived him of true vision is quickly withdrawn from before him. For error, like disease and sleep, long holds fast those who come under its influence; but truth uses the word as a goad, and smites the slumberers, and awakens them; and when they are awake they look at the truth, and also understand it: they hear, and distinguish that which is from that which is not. For there are men who call iniquity righteousness: they think, for example, that it is righteousness for a man to err with the many. But I, for my part, affirm that it is not a good excuse *for error* that a man errs with the many. For, if one man only sin, his sin is great: how much greater will be the sin when many sin *together!*

"Now, the sin of which I speak is this: when a man abandons that which really exists, and serves that which does not really exist. There 'is' that which really exists, and it is called God. He, *I say*, really exists, and by His power doth everything subsist. This being is in no sense made, nor did He ever come into being; but He has existed from eternity, and will *continue to* exist for ever and ever. He changeth not, while everything *else* changes. No eye can see Him, nor thought apprehend Him, nor language describe Him; and those who love Him speak of Him thus: 'Father, and God of Truth.'

"If, therefore, a man forsake the light, and say that there is another God, it is plain from what he himself says that it is some created thing which he calls God. For, if a man call fire God, it is not God, because it is fire; and, if a man call water God, it is not God, because it is water; and, if *he so call* this earth on which we tread, or these heavens which are seen by us, or the sun, or the moon, or some one of these stars which run their course without ceasing by *Divine* command, and do not speed along by their own will, *neither are these gods;* and, if a man call gold and silver gods, are not these objects things which we use as we please? and, if *he so call* those pieces of wood which we burn, or those stones which we break, how can these things be gods? For, lo! they are *for* the use of man. How can 'they' escape the commission of great sin, who in their speech change the great God into those things which, so long as they continue, continue by *Divine* command?

"But, notwithstanding this, I say that so long as a man does not hear, and *so* does not discern or understand that there is a Lord over these creatures, he is not perhaps to be blamed: because no one finds fault with a blind man though he walk ever so badly. For, in the same manner *as the blind, so* men also, when they were seeking after God, stumbled upon stones and blocks of wood; and such of them as were rich stumbled upon gold and silver, and were prevented by their stumblings from *finding* that which they were seeking after. But, now that a voice has been heard through all the earth, *declaring* that there is a God of truth, and there has been given to every man an eye wherewith to see, those persons are without excuse who are ashamed of *incurring the censure of* their former companions in error, and yet desire to walk in the right way. For those who are ashamed to be saved must of necessity perish. I therefore counsel them to open their eyes and see: for, lo! light is given abundantly to us all to see thereby; and if, when light has arisen upon us, any one close his eyes so as not to see, into the ditch he must go. But why is a man ashamed of *the censure of* those who have been in error along with himself? Rather does it behove him to persuade them to follow in his steps; and, if they should not be persuaded by him, *then* to disengage himself from their society. For there are some men who are unable to rise from their mother earth, and therefore also do they make them gods. from the earth their mother; and they are condemned by the judgments of truth, forasmuch as they apply the name *of Him* who is unchangeable to those objects which are subject to change, and shrink not from calling those things gods which have been made by the hands of man, and dare to make an image of God whom they have not seen.

"But I *have to* remark further, that the Sibyl also has said concerning them that it is the images of deceased kings that they worship. And this is easy to understand: for, lo! even now they worship and honour the images of those of Caesarean rank more than their former gods; for from those their former *gods* both *pecuniary* tribute and produce accrue to Caesar, as to one who is greater than they. On this account, those who despise them, and *so* cause Caesar's revenue to fall short, are put to death. But to the treasury of other kings also it is appointed how much the worshippers in various places shall pay, and how many vesselfuls of water from the sea they shall supply. Such is the wickedness of the world-of those who worship and fear that which has no sensation. Many of them, too, who are crafty, either for the sake of gain, or for vainglory, or for dominion over the multitude, both themselves worship, and incite those who are destitute of understanding to worship, that which has no sensation.

"I will further write and show, as far as my ability goes, how and for what causes images were made to kings and tyrants, and *how* they came to be regarded as gods. The people of Argos made images to Hercules, because he belonged to their city, and was strong, and by his valour slew noxious beasts, and more especially because they were afraid of him. For he was subject to no control, and carried off the wives of many: for his lust was great, like that of Zuradi the Persian, his friend. Again, the people of Acre worshipped Dionysus, a king, because he had recently planted the vine in their country. The Egyptians worshipped Joseph the Hebrew, who was called Serapis, because he supplied them with corn during the years of famine. The Athenians worshipped Athene, the daughter of Zeus, king of the island of Crete, because she built the town of Athens, and made Ericthippus her son king there, whom she had by adultery with Hephaestus, a blacksmith, son of a wife of her father. She was, too, always courting the society of Hercules, because he was her brother on her father's side. For Zeus the king became enamoured of Alcmene, the wife of Electryon, who was from Argos, and committed adultery with her, and she gave birth to Hercules. The people of Phoenicia worshipped Balthi, queen of Cyprus, because she fell in love with Tamuz, son of

Cuthar king of the Phoenicians, and left her own kingdom and came and dwelt in Gebal, a fortress of the Phoenicians, and at the same time made all the Cyprians subject to King Cuthar. Also, before Tamuz she had fallen in love with Ares, and committed adultery with him; and Hephaestus, her husband, caught her, and his jealousy was roused against her, and he came and killed Tamuz in Mount Lebanon, as he was hunting wild boars; and from that time Balthi remained in Gebal, and she died in the city of Aphiki, where Tamuz was buried. The Elamites worshipped Nuh, daughter of the king of Elam: when the enemy had carried her captive, her father made for her an image and a temple in Shushan, a royal residence which is in Elam. The Syrians worshipped Athi, a Hadibite, who sent the daughter of Belat, a person skilled in medicine, and she healed Simi, the daughter of Hadad king of Syria; and some time afterwards, when Hadad himself had the leprosy upon him, Athi entreated Elisha the Hebrew, and he came and healed him of his leprosy. The people of Mesopotamia also worshipped Cuthbi, a Hebrew woman, because she delivered Bakru, the paternal *king* of Edessa, from his enemies. With respect to Nebo, who is *worshipped* in Mabug, why should I write to you? For, lo! all the priests who are in Mabug know that it is the image of Orpheus, a Thracian Magus. Hadran, again, is the image of Zaradusht, a Persian Magus. For both of these Magi practised magic at a well which was in a wood in Mabug, in which was an unclean spirit, and it assaulted and disputed the passage of every one who passed by in all that country in which the town of Mabug is situated; and these Magi, in accordance with what was a mystery in their Magian system, bade Simi, the daughter of Hadad, to draw water from the sea and pour it into the well, so that the spirit should not come up and commit assault. In like manner, the rest of mankind made images to their kings and worshipped them; of which matter I will not write further.

"But thou, a *person of* liberal mind, and familiar with the truth, if thou wilt *properly* consider these matters, commune with thine own self; and, though they should clothe thee in the garb of a woman, remember that thou art a man. Believe in Him who is in reality God, and to Him lay open thy mind, and to Him commit thy soul, and He is able to give thee immortal life for ever, for everything is possible to Him; and let all other things be esteemed by thee just as they are-images as images, and sculptures as sculptures; and let not that which is only made be put by thee in the place of Him who is not made, but let Him, the ever-living God, be constantly present to thy mind. For thy mind itself is His likeness: for it too is invisible and impalpable, and not to be represented by any form, yet by its will is the whole bodily frame moved. Know, therefore, that, if thou constantly serve Him who is immoveable, even He exists for ever, so thou also, when thou shalt have put off this *body*, which is visible and corruptible, shall stand before Him for ever, endowed with life and knowledge, and thy works shall be to thee wealth inexhaustible and possessions unfailing. And know that the chief of thy good works is this: that thou know God, and serve Him. Know, too, that He asketh not anything of thee: He needeth not anything.

"Who is this God? He who is Himself truth, and His word truth. And what is truth? That which is not fashioned, nor made, nor represented by art: that is, which has never been brought into existence, and is *on that account* called truth. If, therefore, a man worship that which is made with hands, it is not the truth that he worships, nor yet the word of truth.

"I have very much to say on this subject; but I feel ashamed for those who do not understand that they are superior to the work of their own hands, nor perceive how they give gold to the artists that they may make for them gods, and give them silver for their adornment and honour, and move their riches about from place to place, and *then* worship them. And what infamy can be greater than this, that a man should worship his riches, and forsake Him who bestowed those riches upon him? and that he should revile man, yet worship the image of man; and slay a beast, yet worship the likeness of a beast?

This also is evident, that it is the workmanship of their fellowmen that they worship: for they do not worship the treasures while they are laid by in the bag, but when the artists have fashioned images out of them they worship them; neither do they worship the gold or the silver considered as property, but when the gravers have sculptured them then they worship them. Senseless man to what addition has been made to thy gold, that now thou worshippest it? If it is because it has been made to resemble a winged animal, why dost thou not worship the winged animal *itself*? And if because it has been made like a beast of prey, lo! the beast of prey itself is before thee. And if it is the workmanship itself that pleases thee, let the workmanship of God please thee, who made all things, and in His own likeness made the workmen, who strive to do like Him, but resemble Him not.

"But perhaps thou wilt say: How is it that God did not so make me that I should serve Him, and not images? In speaking thus, thou art seeking to become an idle instrument, and not a living man. For God made thee as perfect as it seemed good to Him. He has given thee a mind endowed with freedom; He has set before thee objects in great number, that thou on thy part mayest distinguish *the nature of* each thing and choose for thyself that which is good: He has set before thee the heavens, and placed in them the stars; He has set before thee the sun and the moon, and they too every day run their course therein; He has set before thee the multitude of waters, and restrained them by His word; He has set before thee the wide earth, which remains at rest, and continues before thee without variation: yet, lest thou shouldst suppose that of its own nature it *so* continues, He makes it also to quake when He pleaseth; He has set before thee the clouds, which by *His* command bring water from above and satisfy the earth-that from hence thou mayest understand that He who puts these things in motion is superior to them all, and mayest accept *thankfully* the goodness of Him who has given thee a mind whereby to distinguish these things from one another.

"Wherefore I counsel thee to know thyself, and to know God. For understand how that there is within thee that which is called the soul-by it the eye seeth, by it the ear heareth, by it the mouth speaketh; and how it makes use of the whole body; and *how*, whenever He pleaseth to remove the soul from the body, this falleth *to decay* and perisheth. From this, therefore, which exists within thyself and is invisible, understand how God also moveth the whole by His power, like the body; and that, whenever it pleases Him to withdraw His power, the whole world also, like the body, will fall *to decay* and perish.

"But why this world was made, and why it passes away, and why the body exists, and why it falls *to decay*, and why it continues, thou canst not know

Melito of Sardis

until thou hast raised thy head from this sleep in which thou art sunk, and hast opened thine eyes and seen that God is One, the Lord of all, and hast come to serve Him with all thy heart. Then will He grant thee to know His will: for every one that is severed from the knowledge of the living God is dead and buried *even while* in his body. Therefore *is it that* thou dost wallow on the ground before demons and shadows, and askest vain petitions from that which has not anything to give. But thou, stand thou up from among those who are lying on the earth and caressing stones, and giving their substance as food for the fire, and offering their raiment to idols, and; while *themselves* possessed of senses, are bent on serving that which has no sensation; and offer thou for thy imperishable soul petitions *far that* which decayeth not, to God who suffers no decay-and thy freedom will be at once apparent; and be thou careful of it, and give thanks to God who made thee, and gave thee the mind of the free, that thou mightest shape thy conduct even as thou wilt. He hath set before thee all these things, and showeth thee that, if thou follow after evil, thou shall be condemned for thy evil deeds; but that, if after goodness, thou shall receive from Him abundant good, together with immortal life for ever.
"There is, therefore, nothing to hinder thee from changing thy evil manner of life, because thou art a free man; or from seeking and finding out who is the

Lord of all; or from serving Him with all thy heart: because with Him there is no reluctance to give the knowledge of Himself to those that seek it, according to the measure of their capacity to know Him.

"Let it be thy first care not to deceive thyself. For, if thou sayest of that which is not God: This is God, thou deceivest thyself, and sinnest before the God of truth. Thou fool I is that God which is *bought and sold?* Is that God which is in want? Is that God which must be watched over? How buyest thou him as a slave, and servest him as a master? How askest thou of him, as of one that is rich, to give to thee, and thyself givest to him as to one that is poor? How dost thou expect of him that he will make thee victorious in battle? for, lo! when thy enemies have conquered thee, they strip him likewise.

"Perhaps one who is a king may say: I cannot behave myself aright, because I am a king; it becomes me to do the will of the many. He who speaks thus really deserves to be laughed at: for why should not the king himself lead the way to all good things, and persuade the people under his rule to behave with purity, and to know God in truth, and in his own person set before them the patterns of all things excellent-since thus it becomes him to do? For it is a shameful thing that a king, however badly he may conduct himself, should *yet* judge and condemn those who do amiss.

Melito of Sardis

"My opinion is this: that in 'this' way a kingdom may be governed in peace-when the sovereign is acquainted with the God of truth, and is withheld by fear of Him from doing wrong to those who are his subjects, and judges everything with equity, as one who knows that he himself also will be judged before God; while, at the same time, those who are under his rule are withheld by the fear of God from doing wrong to their sovereign, and are restrained by *the same* fear from doing wrong to one another. By this knowledge of God and fear of Him all evil may be removed from the realm. For, if the sovereign abstain from doing wrong to those who are under his rule, and they abstain from doing wrong to him and to each other, it is evident that the whole country will dwell in peace. Many blessings, too, will be *enjoyed* there, because amongst them all the name of God will be glorified. For what blessing is greater than this, that a sovereign should deliver the people that are under his rule from error, and by this good deed render himself pleasing to God? For from error arise all those evils *from which kingdoms suffer;* but the greatest of all errors is this: when a man is ignorant of God, and in God's stead worships that which is not God.

"There are, however, persons who say: It is for the honour of God that we make the image: in order, that is, that we may worship the God who is concealed from our view. But they are unaware that

God is in every country, and in every place, and is never absent, and that there is not anything done and He knoweth it not. Yet thou, despicable man! within whom He is, and without whom He is, and above whom He is, hast nevertheless gone and bought thee wood from the carpenter's, and it is carved and made into an image insulting to God. To this thou offerest sacrifice, and knowest not that the all-seeing eye seeth thee, and that the word of truth reproves thee, and says to thee: How can the unseen God be sculptured? Nay, it is the likeness of thyself that thou makest and worshippest. Because the wood has been sculptured, hast thou not the insight to perceive that it is *still* wood, or *that the stone* is *still* stone? The gold also the workman taketh according to its weight in the balance. And when thou hast had it made into an image, why dose thou weigh it? Therefore thou art a lover of gold, and not a lover of God. And art thou not ashamed, perchance it be deficient, to demand of the maker of it why he has stolen some of it? Though thou hast eyes, dose thou not see? And though thou hast intelligence, dose thou not understand? Why dose thou wallow on the ground, and offer supplication to things which are without sense? Fear Him who shaketh the earth, and maketh the heavens to revolve, and smiteth the sea, and removeth the mountain from its place-Him who can make Himself like a fire, and consume all things; and, if thou be not able to clear thyself of guilt, yet add not to thy sins; and, if thou be not able to know God, yet doubt not that He exists.

"Again, there are persons who say: Whatsoever our fathers have bequeathed to us, *that* we reverence. Therefore, of course, it is, that those whose fathers have bequeathed them poverty strive to become rich! and those whose fathers did not instruct them, desire to be instructed, and to learn that which their fathers knew not! And why, forsooth, do the children of the blind see, and the children of the lame walk? Nay, it is not well for a man to follow *his* predecessors, *if they be* those whose course was evil; but *rather* that we should turn from that path of theirs, lest that which befell *our* predecessors should bring disaster upon us also. Wherefore, inquire whether thy father's course was good: and, *if so*, do thou also follow in his steps; but, if thy father's course was very evil, let thine be good, and so let it be with thy children after thee. Be grieved also for thy father because his course is evil, so long as thy grief may avail to help him. But, as for thy children, speak to them thus: There is a God, the Father of all, who never came into being, neither was ever made, and by whose will all things subsist. He also made the luminaries, that His works may see one another; and He conceals Himself in His power from all His works; for it is not permitted to any being subject to change to see Him who changes not. But such as are mindful *of His words*, and are admitted into that covenant which is unchangeable, 'they' see God-so far as it is possible for them to see Him. These also will have power to escape destruction, when the flood of fire comes upon all the world. For there was once a flood and a wind, and the great men were swept away by a violent blast from the north, but the just were left, for a demonstration of the truth. Again, at another time there was a flood of water, and all men and animals perished in the multitude of waters, but the just were preserved in an ark of wood by the command of God. So also will it be at the last time: there shall be a flood of fire, and the earth shall be burnt up, together with its mountains; and mankind shall be burnt up, along with the idols which they have made, and the carved images which they have worshipped; and the sea shall be burnt up, together with its islands; but the just shall be preserved from wrath, like as *were* their fellows of the ark from the waters of the deluge. And then shall those who have not known God, and those who have made them idols, bemoan themselves, when they shall see those idols of theirs being burnt up, together with themselves, and nothing shall be found to help them.

"When thou, Antoninus Caesar, shall become acquainted with these things, and thy children also with thee, *then* wilt thou bequeath to them an inheritance for ever which fadeth not away, and thou wilt deliver thy soul, and the souls of thy children

Melito of Sardis

also, from that which shall come. upon the whole earth in the judgment of truth *and* of righteousness. For, according as thou hast acknowledged Him here, *so* will He acknowledge thee there; and, if thou account Him here superfluous, He will not account thee one of those who have known Him and confessed Him.

"These *may* suffice thy Majesty; and, if they be *too* many, yet deign to accept them." *Here* endeth Melito.

II.
- From the Discourse on Soul and Body.

For this reason did the Father send His Son from heaven without a bodily form, that, when He should put on a body by means of the Virgin's womb, and be born man, He might save man, and gather together those members of His which death had scattered when he divided man.

And further on: -The earth shook, and its foundations trembled; the sun fled away, and the elements turned back, and the day was changed *into night:* for they could not endure *the sight of* their Lord hanging on a tree. The *whole* creation was amazed, marvelling and saying, "What new mystery, then, is this? The Judge is judged, and holds his peace; the Invisible One is seen, and is not ashamed; the Incomprehensible is laid hold upon, and is not indignant; the Illimitable is circumscribed, and doth not resist; the Impossible suffereth, and doth not avenge; the Immortal dieth, and answereth not a word; the Celestial is laid in the grave, and endureth! What new mystery is this? "The *whole* creation, I *say*, was astonished; but, when our Lord arose from the place of the dead, and trampled death under foot, and bound the strong one, and set man free, then did the whole creation see clearly that for man's sake the Judge was condemned, and the Invisible was seen, and the Illimitable was circumscribed, and the Impassible suffered, and the Immortal died, and the Celestial was laid in the gave. For our Lord, when He was born man, was condemned in order that He might Show mercy, was bound in order that He might loose, was seized in order that He might release, suffered in order that He might feel compassion, died in order that He might give life, was laid in the grave that He might raise *from the dead.*

III.
- From the Discourse on the Cross.

On these accounts He came to us; on these accounts, though He was incorporeal, He formed for Himself a body after our fashion, -appearing as a sheep, yet still remaining the Shepherd; being esteemed a servant, yet not renouncing the Sonship; being carried *in the womb* of Mary, yet arrayed in *the nature of* His Father; treading upon the earth, yet filling heaven; appearing as an infant, yet not discarding the eternity of His nature; being invested with a body, yet not circumscribing the unmixed simplicity of His Godhead; being esteemed poor, yet not divested of His riches; needing sustenance inasmuch as He was man, yet not ceasing to feed the entire world inasmuch as He is God; putting on the likeness of a servant, yet not impairing the likeness of His Father. He sustained every character *belonging to Him* in an immutable nature: He was standing before Pilate, and *at the same time* was sitting with His Father; He was nailed upon the tree, and *yet* was the Lord of all things.

IV.
- On Faith.

We have collected together *extracts* from the Law and the Prophets relating to those things which have Been declared concerning our Lord Jesus Christ, that we may prove to your love that this *Being* is perfect reason, the Word of God; He who was begotten before the light; He who is Creator together with the Father; He who is the Fashioner of man; He who is all in all; He who among the patriarchs is Patriarch; He who in the law is the Law; among the priests, Chief Priest; among kings, the Ruler; among prophets, the Prophet; among the angels, Archangel; in the voice *of the preacher*, the Word; among spirits, the Spirit; in the Father, the Son; in God, God; King for ever and ever. For this is He who was pilot to

Noah; He who was guide to Abraham; He who was bound with Isaac; He who was in exile with Jacob; He who was sold with Joseph; He who was captain of the host with Moses; He who was the divider of the inheritance with Jesus the son of Nun; He who in David and the prophets announced His own sufferings; He who put on a bodily form in the Virgin; He who was born in Bethlehem; He who was wrapped in swaddling-clothes in the manger; He who was seen by the shepherds; He who was glorified by the angels; He who was worshipped by the Magi; He who was pointed out by John; He who gathered together the apostles; He who preached the kingdom; He who cured the lame; He who gave light to the blind; He who raised the dead; He who appeared in the temple; He who was not believed on by the people; He who was betrayed by Judas; He who was apprehended by the priests; He who was condemned by Pilate; He who was pierced in the flesh; He who was hanged on the tree; He who was buried in the earth; He who rose from the place of the dead; He who appeared to the apostles; He who was carried up to heaven; He who is seated at the right hand of the Father; He who is the repose of those that are departed; the recoverer of those that are lost; the light of those that are in darkness; the deliverer of those that are captive; the guide of those that go astray; the asylum of the afflicted; the bridegroom of the Church; the charioteer of the cherubim; the captain of the angels; God who is from God; the Son who is from the Father; Jesus Christ the King for evermore. Amen.

V.
This is He who took a bodily form in the Virgin, and was hanged upon the tree, and was buried within the earth, and suffered not dissolution; He who rose from the place of the dead, and raised up men from the earth-from the grave below to the height of heaven. This is the Lamb that was slain; this is the Lamb that opened not His mouth. This is He who was born of Mary, fair sheep *of the fold*. This is He that was taken from the flock, and was led to the slaughter, and was slain in the evening, and was buried at night; He who had no bone of Him broken on the tree; He who suffered not dissolution within the earth; He who rose from the place of the dead, and raised up the race of Adam from the grave below, This is He who was put to death. And where was He put to death? In the midst of Jerusalem. By whom? By Israel: became He cured their lame, and cleansed their lepers, and gave light to their blind, and raised their dead! This was the cause of His death. Thou, *O Israel*, wast giving commands, and He was being crucified; thou wast rejoicing, and He was being buried; thou wast reclining on a soft couch, and He was watching in the grave and the shroud. O Israel, transgressor of the law, why hast

thou committed this new iniquity, subjecting the Lord to new sufferings-thine own Lord, Him who fashioned thee, Him-who made thee, Him who honoured thee, who called thee Israel? But thou hast not been found to be Israel: for thou hast not seen God, nor understood the Lord. Thou hast not known, O Israel, that this was the first-born of God, who was begotten before the sun, who made the light to shine forth, who lighted up the day, who separated the darkness, who fixed the first foundations, who poised the earth, who collected the ocean, who stretched out the firmament, who adorned the world. Bitter *were* thy nails, and sharp; bitter thy tongue, which thou didst whet; bitter *was* Judas, to whom thou gavest hire; bitter thy false witnesses, whom thou stirredst up; bitter thy gall, which thou preparedst; bitter thy vinegar, which thou madest; bitter thy hands, filled with blood. Thou slewest thy Lord, and He was lifted up upon the tree; and an inscription was fixed *above*, to show who He was that was slain. And who was this? (that which we shall not say is *too* shocking *to hear*, and that which we shall say is very dreadful: nevertheless hearken, and tremble.) *It was* He because of whom the earth quaked. He that hung up the earth *in space* was *Himself* hanged up; He that fixed the heavens was fixed *with nails;* He that bore up the earth was borne up on a tree; the Lord *of all* was subjected to ignominy in a naked body-God put to death! the

Melito of Sardis

King of Israel slain with Israel's right hand! Alas for the new wickedness of the new murder! The Lord was exposed with naked body: He was not deemed worthy even of covering; and, in order that He might not be seen, the luminaries turned away, and the day became darkened because they slew God, who hung naked on the tree. It was not the body of our Lord that the luminaries covered with darkness when they set, but the eyes of men. For, because the people quaked not, the earth quaked; because they were not affrighted, the earth was affrighted. Thou smotest thy Lord: thou also hast been smitten upon the earth. And thou indeed liest dead; but He is risen from the place of the dead, and ascended to the height of heaven, having suffered for the sake of those who suffer, and having been bound for the sake of Adam's race which was imprisoned, and having been judged for the sake of him who was condemned, and having been buried for the sake of him who was buried.

And further on: -This is He who made the heaven and the earth, and in the beginning, together with the Father, fashioned man; who was announced by means of the law and the prophets; who put on a bodily form in the Virgin; who was hanged upon the tree; who was buried in the earth; who rose from the place of the dead, and ascended to the height of heaven, and sitteth on the right hand of the Father.
VI.

He that bore up the earth was borne up on a tree. The Lord was subjected to ignominy with naked body-God put to death, the King of Israel slain!

- Fragments.

I.
From the work on the passover. When Servilius Paulus was proconsul of Asia, at the time that Sagaris suffered martyrdom, there arose a great controversy at Laodicea concerning the time of the celebration of the Passover, which on that occasion had happened to fall at the proper season; and this *treatise* was *then* written.

II.
- *From the apology addressed to Marcus Aurelius Antoninus.*

For the race of the pious is now persecuted in a way contrary to all precedent, being harassed by a new kind of edicts everywhere in Asia. For unblushing informers, and such as are greedy of other men's goods, taking occasion from the orders *issued*, carry on their robbery without any disguise, plundering of their property night and day those who are guilty of no wrong.

If these proceedings take place at thy bidding, well and good. For a just sovereign will never take unjust measures; and we, on our part, gladly accept the honour of such a death. This request only we present

Melito of Sardis

to thee, that thou wouldst first of all examine for thyself into the behaviour of these *reputed* agents of so much strife, and then come to a just decision as to whether they merit death and punishment, or deserve to live in safety and quiet. But if, on the contrary, it shall turn out that this measure, and this new sort of command, which it would be unbecoming to employ even against barbarian foemen, do not proceed from thee, then all the more do we entreat thee not to leave us thus exposed to the spoliation of the populace.

For the philosophy current with us flourished in the first instance among barbarians; and, when it afterwards sprang up among the nations under thy rule, during the distinguished reign of thy ancestor Augustus, it proved to be a blessing of most happy omen to thy empire. For from that time the Roman power has risen to greatness and splendour. To this power thou hast succeeded as the much desired possessor; and such shalt thou continue, together with thy son, if thou protect that philosophy which has grown up with thy empire, and which took its rise with Augustus; to which also thy *more recent* ancestors paid honour, along with the other religions *prevailing in the empire*. A very strong proof, moreover, that it was for good that the system we profess came to prevail at the same time that the empire of such happy commencement was established, is this-that ever since the reign of

Augustus nothing untoward has happened; but, on the contrary, everything has contributed to the splendour and renown *of the empire*, in accordance with the devout wishes of all. Nero and Domitian alone of all *the emperors*, imposed upon by certain calumniators, have cared to bring any impeachment against our doctrines. They, too, are the source from which it has happened that the lying slanders on those who profess them have, in consequence of the senseless habit which prevails *of taking things on hear*say, flowed down to our own times. But the course which they in their ignorance pursued was set aside by thy pious progenitors, who frequently and in many instances rebuked by their rescripts those who dared to set on foot any hostilities against them. It appears, for example, that thy grandfather Adrian wrote, among others, to Fundanus, the proconsul then in charge of the government of Asia. Thy father, too, when thou thyself wast associated with him in the administration of the empire, wrote to the cities, forbidding them to take any measures adverse to us: among the rest to the people of Larissa, and of Thessalonica, and of Athens, and, *in short*, to all the Greeks. And as regards thyself, seeing that thy sentiments respecting the Christians are not only the same as theirs, but even much more generous and wise, we are the more persuaded that thou wilt do all that we ask of thee.

III.
- *From the same apology.*

We are not those who pay homage to stones, that are without sensation; but of the only God, who is before all and over all, and, moreover, we are worshippers of His Christ, who is veritably God the Word *existing* before all time.

IV.
- *From the Book of Extracts.*

Melito to his brother Onesimus, greeting:-

As you have often, prompted by your regard for the word *of God*, expressed a wish to have some extracts made from the Law and the Prophets concerning the Saviour, and concerning our faith in general, and have desired, moreover, to obtain an accurate account of the Ancient Books, as regards their number and their arrangement, I have striven to the best of my ability to perform this task: well knowing your zeal for the faith, and your eagerness to become acquainted with the Word, and especially because *I am assured that*, through your yearning after God, you esteem these things beyond all things else, engaged as you are in a struggle for eternal salvation.

I accordingly proceeded to the East, and went to the very spot where *the things in question* were preached and took place; and, having made myself accurately acquainted with the books of the Old Testament, I have set them down below, and herewith send you *the list*. Their names are as follows:-

The five *books* of Moses-Genesis, Exodus, Leviticus, Numbers, Deuteronomy; Joshua, Judges, Ruth, the four *books* of Kings, the two of Chronicles, the *book of the* Psalms of David, the Proverbs of Solomon, also called *the Book of* Wisdom, Ecclesiastes, the Song of Songs, Job, *the books of* the prophets Isaiah, Jeremiah, of the twelve contained in a single book, Daniel, Ezekiel, Esdras. From these I have made my extracts, dividing them into six books.

V.
- *From the Catena on Genesis.*

In place of Isaac the just, a ram appeared for slaughter, in order that Isaac might be liberated from *his* bonds. The slaughter of this animal redeemed Isaac *from death*. In like manner, the Lord, being slain, saved us; being bound, He loosed us; being sacrificed, He redeemed us ...

For the Lord was a lamb, like the ram which Abraham saw caught in the bush Sabec. But this bush represented the cross, and that place Jerusalem, and the lamb the Lord bound for slaughter.

For as a ram was He bound, says he concerning our Lord Jesus Christ, and as a lamb was He shorn, and as a sheep was He led to the slaughter, and as a lamb was He crucified; and He carried the cross on His shoulders when He was led up *to the hill* to be slain, as was Isaac by his father. But Christ suffered, and Isaac did not suffer: for he was *but* a type of Him who should suffer. Yet, even when serving only for a type of Christ, he smote men with astonishment and fear.

For a new mystery was presented to view,-a son led by his father to a mountain to be slain, whose feet he bound together, and laid him on the wood of the sacrifice, preparing with care whatever was necessary to his immolation. Isaac on his part is silent, bound like a ram, not opening his mouth, nor uttering a sound with his voice. For, not fearing the knife, nor quailing before the fire, nor troubled by *the prospect of* suffering, he sustained bravely *the character of* the type of the Lord. Accordingly there lies Isaac before us, with his feet bound like a ram, his father standing by, with the knife all bare in his hand, not shrinking from shedding the blood of his son.

VI.

- *Two scholia on Genesis 22:13.*

The Syriac and the Hebrew use the word "suspended," as more clearly typifying the cross.

The word Sabek some have rendered *remission*, others *upright*, as if the meaning, agreeing with the popular belief, were-a goat walking erect up to a bush, and there standing erect caught by his horns, so as to be a plain type of the cross. For this reason it is not translated, because the single Hebrew word signifies in other languages many things. To those, however, who ask it is proper to give an answer, and to say that Sabek denotes *lifted up*.

VII.
- *On the nature of Christ.*

For there is no need, to persons of intelligence, to attempt to prove, from the deeds of Christ subsequent to His baptism, that His soul and His body, His human nature like ours, were real, and no phantom of the imagination. For the deeds done by Christ after His baptism, and especially His miracles, gave indication and assurance to the world of the Deity hidden in His flesh. For, being at once both God and perfect man likewise, He gave us sure indications of His two natures: of His Deity, by His miracles during the three years that elapsed after His baptism; of His humanity, during the thirty *similar* periods which preceded His baptism, in which, by reason of His low estate as regards the flesh, He concealed the signs of His Deity, although He was the true God existing before all ages.

VIII.
- *From the Oration on Our Lord's Passion.*

God has suffered from the right hand of Israel.

IX.

Head of the Lord-His simple Divinity; because He is the Beginning and Creator of all things: in Daniel.

The white hair of the Lord, because He is "the Ancient of Days: "as above.

The eyes of the Lord-the Divine inspection: because He sees all things. Like that in the apostle: For all things are naked and open in His eyes."

*The eyelids of the*Lord-hidden spiritual mysteries in the Divine precepts. In the Psalm: "His eyelids question, that is prove, the children of men."

The smelling of the Lord-His delight in the prayers or works of the saints. In Genesis: "And the Lord smelled an odour of sweetness."

The mouth of the Lord-His Son, or word *addressed* to men. In the prophet, "The mouth of the Lord hath spoken; " and elsewhere, "They provoked His mouth to anger."

The tongue of the Lord-His Holy Spirit. In the Psalm: "My tongue is a pen."

The face of the Lord-His manifestation. In Exodus, "My face shall go before thee; " and in the prophet, "The face of the Lord divided them."

The word of the Lord-His Son. In the Psalm: "My heart hath uttered a good word."

The arm of the Lord-His Son, by whom He hath wrought all His works. In the prophet Isaiah: "And to whom is the arm of the Lord revealed? "

The right hand of the Lord-that is, *His* Son; as also above in the Psalm: "The right hand of the Lord hath done valiantly."

The right hand of the Lord-*electio omnis*. As in Deuteronomy: "In His right hand *is* a fiery law."

The wings of the Lord-Divine protection. In the Psalm: "In the shadow of Thy wings will I hope."

The shoulder of the Lord-the Divine power, by which He condescends to carry the feeble. In Deuteronomy: "He took them up, and put them on His shoulders."

The hand of the Lord-Divine operation. In the prophet: "Have not my hands made all these things?"

The finger of the Lord-the Holy Spirit, by whose operation the tables of the law in Exodus are said to have been written; and in the Gospel: "If I by the finger of God cast out demons"

The fingers of the Lord-The lawgiver Moses, or the prophets. In the Psalm: "I will regard the heavens," that is, the books of the Law and the Prophets, "the works of Thy fingers."

The wisdom of the Lord-His Son. In the apostle: "Christ the power of God, and the wisdom of God; " and in Solomon: "The wisdom of the Lord reacheth from one end to the other mightily."

The womb of the Lord-the hidden recess of Deity out of which He brought forth His Son. In the Psalm:

"Out of the womb, before Lucifer, have I borne Thee.
The feet of the Lord-His immoveableness and eternity. In the Psalm: "And thick darkness was under His feet."
The throne of the Lord-angels, or saints, or simply sovereign dominion. In the Psalm: "Thy throne, O God, is for ever and ever."
Seat-the same as above, angels or saints, because the Lord sits upon these. In the Psalm: "The Lord sat upon His holy seat."
The descent of the Lord-His visitation of men. As in Micah: "Behold, the Lord shall come forth from His place; He shall come down trampling under foot the ends of the earth." Likewise in a bad sense. In Genesis: "The Lord came down to see the tower."
The ascent of the Lord-the raising up of man, who is taken from earth to heaven. In the Psalm: "Who ascendeth above the heaven of heavens to the east."
The standing of the Lord-the patience of the Deity, by which He bears with sinners that they may come to repentance. As in Habakkuk: "He good and measured the earth; and in the Gospel: "Jesus stood, and bade him be called," that is, the blind man.
The transition of the Lord-His assumption of our flesh, through which by His birth, His death, His resurrection, His ascent into heaven, He made transitions, so to say. In the Song of Songs: "Behold,

He cometh, leaping upon the mountains, bounding over the hills."

The going of the Lord-His coming or visitation. In the Psalm.

The way of the Lord-the operation of the Deity. As in Job, in speaking of the devil: "He is the beginning of the ways of the Lord."

Again: *The ways of the Lord*-His precepts. In Hosea: "For the ways of the Lord are straight, and the just shall walk in them."

The footsteps of the Lord-the signs of *His* secret operations. As in the Psalm: "And Thy footsteps shall not be known."

The knowledge of the Lord-that which makes men to know Him. To Abraham *He says:* "Now I know that thou fearest the Lord; " that is, I have made thee to know.

The ignorance of God is His disapproval. In the Gospel: "I know you not."

The remembrance of God-His mercy, by which He rejects and has mercy on whom He will. So in Genesis: "The Lord remembered Noah; " and in another passage: "The Lord hath remembered His people."

The repentance of the Lord-His change of procedure. As in the book of Kings: "It repented me that I have made Saul king."

The anger and wrath of the Lord-the vengeance of the Deity upon sinners, when He bears with them with a view to punishment, does not *at once* judge them according to *strict* equity. As in the Psalm: "In His anger and in His wrath will He trouble them."

The sleeping of the Lord-when, in the thoughts of some, His faithfulness is not sufficiently wakeful. In the Psalm: "Awake, why sleepest Thou, O Lord?"

The watches of the Lord-in the guardianship of His elect He is always at hand by the presence of *His* Deity. In the Psalm: "Lo! He will not slumber nor sleep."

The sitting of the Lord-His ruling. In the Psalm: "The Lord sitteth upon His holy seat."

The footstool of the Lord-man assumed by the Word; or His saints, as some think. In the Psalm: "Worship ye His footstool, for it is holy."

The walking of the Lord-the delight of the Deity in the walks of His elect. In the prophet: "I will walk in them, and will be their Lord."

The trumpet of the Lord-His mighty voice. In the apostle: "At the command, and at the voice of the archangel, and at the trumpet of God, shall He descend from heaven."

Made in the USA
Monee, IL
26 November 2022